Surrey Privies

by

John Janaway

COUNTRYSIDE BOOKS

NEWBURY • BERKSHIRE

First published 1999

COUNTRYSIDE BOOKS
3 Catherine Road
Newbury, Berkshire

ISBN 1 85306 545 5

Produced through MRM Associates Ltd., Reading
Printed by Woolnough Bookbinding Ltd., Irthlingborough

Contents

FOREWORD

Privy hunting is a curious occupation. You may find yourself marching up the path of a well manicured garden, knocking on the front door of someone you have never met and asking if you can see their privy. But imagine it from the other side of the door! You answer your front door to be confronted by a complete stranger, who says that he has been told by a friend or neighbour that there might be a long lost privy in your garden! It says a great deal for the pleasant nature and generosity of spirit of so many Surrey people that not once was I told in no uncertain terms to 'clear off'. Although I was sometimes not entirely sure whether the dog that also came to greet me was friend or foe, on most occasions they seemed as enthusiastic about my quest for privies as their owners!

I am not able to claim first hand experience of that chilly walk to the bottom of the garden on a dark night, clutching a torch or candle, with yesterday's newspaper tucked under the arm. I was brought up to think that the warm comfort of an indoor flush loo was the norm. As a child I had no knowledge that, only a few miles away, many people still had bucket toilets, which were being emptied once a week by the men with the 'lavender van'. Perhaps the nearest I came to a privy was the flush loo at my uncle's farm in Hampshire, which was all of three feet outside the back door! But many beasties and bogeymen haunted those few steps across cold concrete as the back door closed behind me.

My interest in privies began many years ago when I was helping on an archaeological 'dig' in Godalming. There I came across the remains of a little brick 'sentry box' with an unusual archway built into the base of one wall. I came to the conclusion that it was the remains of an old loo but I had no

The author discovers a wooden box designed to hold squares of newspaper. Clearly some privies were not intended for those of above average height! (Roy Drysdale)

idea of how it actually worked. Thereafter, my interest in such 'little houses' lay dormant. I concluded that almost certainly none of them had survived in 'modern' Surrey. But about two years ago I picked up the scent and soon discovered that the Surrey privy was far from extinct! I found, however, that surviving redundant privies were often sadly neglected, whilst many had lost their internal features and now served as garden sheds. I came to realise that this important, indeed essential, aspect of Surrey's social history was in danger of becoming only the faintest footnote in the county's recorded past.

It is obvious that this book could not have been completed without the help of many Surrey people. Special thanks go to Roy Drysdale, who took many of the photographs and accompanied me on several of my expeditions in search of the elusive privy. Thanks also to 'Lootique Len' Blackmore, Chris Shepheard and the Farnham Buildings Preservation Trust, and Mary Pritchard, who also provided photographs. Audrey Monk, Janet Balchin, Philip Gorton, Audrey Graham, Matthew Alexander, Kevin Fryer and John Boas also gave me invaluable and enthusiastic support. Also special thanks to Sheila Ashcroft for putting up with endless talk of privies! Thank you also to the National Trust and to the editors of the *Surrey Advertiser, Surrey Mirror, Surrey Herald, Farnham Herald and Dorking Advertiser.*

I am also very grateful to the following (in no particular order) for allowing me to see their privies or for providing me with their privy memories and other useful information: Mary Gatford, Duncan Mirylees, Ruth Drysdale, David Rose, Henry Jackson, Hugo Russell, Doris Vincent, the late Mr A. Trower and his daughter, Rosalie Vincent, Peter Gellatly, L. Hampshire, Audrey Creasey, Mr D. J. Buxton, Edward Lucas, Miss M. H. Jordan, Anthony Cunningham, Mrs B. J. Bache,

June Spong, Evelyn Browne, Marie Kite, Nichola Eyton-Jones, Mrs M. Grover, Miss M. E. Riddle, Mrs H. Hubbard, Albert Cunningham, Mrs T. Briggs, Alicia Russell, Francis Russell, Gerald and Margaret Jarvis, Pauline Parry, Joan Hardy, Mr and Mrs Peter Hubsch, Mr Blanshard, Mr and Mrs Taylor, Fiona and Paul Greenhalgh, Brian and Joy Brackley, Neil Brackley, Margaret Smith, Mrs Reed, Colin and Sue Beasley at The Merry Harriers, 'Sophie', Roger Swallow, Rosemary Arrow, Mrs Rowling, Barry Morgan, Mr Wilson, Di Day, Liz Wombwell, Irene Vaines, A. Ingold, Pat Reynolds, Roger Thoday, Mrs Bailey and Bernard Polack. There were also many other people who were ready to talk about my subject but whose names I failed to record. If I have left you out, please accept my apologies.

In this book I make no claim to have produced a comprehensive record of Surrey's surviving privies. I have used only a representative selection from my 'privy' files. In addition, I am sure that there are many, many more privies out there, which I have not yet visited but at least some of these will, no doubt, be brought to light following the publication of this book.

I now invite you to light your candle and join me on a trip down the garden path!

JOHN JANAWAY

The perfect place to sit down, relax and read 'Surrey Privies'. (Roy Drysdale)

[1]

Ancient Privies

In our house the marvels of the flush toilet were taken for granted for years. That is until one day, when the pull of the handle brought only a feeble clonk and no water rushed down to sweep away the latest offering. It was several days before this novice amateur plumber was able to effect a repair and that mighty rush of water was heard once more and with it a return to the normal routine of life.

Thousands of years ago, man the hunter suffered no such traumatic disruptions to his daily routine and where to go and what to do with it was never a problem. He simply went as the need arose, just like the animals he hunted. He had no need to hide behind a bush to spare the blushes of companions as coyness with such a basic bodily function is a comparatively recent development. And where to go only became a problem when man the hunter became man the farmer and he began to settle down in small communities. Even then, as long as it was a bow-shot away from his dark, smoke-filled hut, anywhere was still perfectly acceptable.

The ancient Egyptians nearly 5,000 years ago had tough rules concerning sanitation and the Minoans living on the beautiful Mediterranean island of Crete around 2000 BC were masters of sanitary engineering. Their loos had running water and earthenware pans and wooden seats. None of this technology reached the ancient Britons, however, and such quality was not seen here until quite late in the reign of Queen Victoria nearly 4,000 years later.

It was the Romans who undoubtedly introduced the

Britons to the delights of baths, latrines and clean running water. Sewers were most important to the Romans, who had the goddess of sewers, Cloacina, to watch over their drains to make sure that everything flowed smoothly. Some people still remember this goddess as I was reminded only a few years ago when I came across this on the back of a friend's toilet door:

> Fayre Cloacina, goddesse of this playce,
> Daylie resorte of all ye human race;
> Grayciouslie grant my offerings may flowe
> Not rudlie swift nor obstinatelie slowe.

The Romans even had a god of manure, Stercutius, who perhaps had a good working relationship with Cloacina to guarantee supplies!

Going to the loo was very much a social affair in Roman times with public latrines being constructed which could seat many citizens at a time. A good example has survived at Salamis in Northern Cyprus and here more than 40 people could relax on comfortable wooden seats set in a semi-circle over a conduit of running water to carry away their efforts. Those with small bottoms, particularly children, were catered for with smaller holes on one side whilst the most corpulent sat almost opposite.

At Housesteads Roman Fort on Hadrian's Wall in Northumberland 20 troops could be accommodated at a time in their beautifully constructed latrine. Water to flush the system came from large stone tanks or cisterns and drains carried the waste beyond the wall of the fort. A small open channel with flowing water ran in front of the sitters who, having wiped their rears with a small sponge held on a stick, then rinsed it out in the channel. It has often been said

The Roman latrines at Housesteads in Northumberland. Two rows of wooden seats would have been suspended over the channels to the right and left. (Author)

that the Romans used communal sponges but I suspect that each Roman brought their own sponge when answering the call of nature. Encouraged, no doubt, by the sign on the wall extolling them to 'now wash your hands', they then did so in the stone basins provided at each end of the latrine. At Housesteads it is easy to imagine the Roman auxiliaries seated in the latrine at the end of a long day spent guarding the frontiers of the empire, discussing recent events and exchanging the latest gossip.

The Roman grip on Britain began to loosen at the end of the 4th century. However, many Britons had embraced the Roman way of life and they must have maintained their lifestyle for many years after the official withdrawal of Roman troops in the early 5th century. Arguments continue to rage over whether King Arthur really existed. If he did I'm sure

Two garderobe shafts situated high up in the wall of the keep at Guildford Castle. (Roy Drysdale)

that he and his troops must have insisted on properly constructed latrines. The first Saxons arrived in southern England as mercenaries, who were invited in to protect the Romano-Britons. What these first immigrants thought of the sanitary arrangements they found is anybody's guess. What does seem certain though is that they failed to appreciate the luxury of the communal seat and once more anywhere in wood or field became the place to go. Later Saxon arrivals and also Vikings who settled in England sought to improve their sanitary conditions by digging the occasional pit in which to deposit their waste.

Chertsey Abbey was founded in the late 7th century and it was the monks at such establishments who upheld the standards first set in this island by the Romans. Waverley

Abbey near Farnham was the first Cistercian monastery in England and was founded in 1128. The Cistercians invariably built in quiet valleys close to a river, often redirecting the stream to create channels which would efficiently carry away their waste. At Waverley the monks' *dormitorii necessaria* or reredorter was constructed over a drain fed by the clear waters of the adjacent River Wey. The building was originally about 50 feet long and 20 feet wide with a large number of seats, presumably wooden, arranged in a single long row. By the 13th century the number of monks at Waverley had increased considerably and the reredorter was therefore enlarged to cope with the extra demand. There were now two rows of seats constructed back to back over the drain. Later the number of monks declined so the size of the reredorter was reduced back to its original capacity.

At the time when the monks of Waverley Abbey were enjoying facilities beyond the comprehension of the average villein or serf, the aristocracy had also come to appreciate something better than an unprotected hole in the ground. Tiny rooms or garderobes were often built into the thickness of castle walls above a shaft. A seat or seats with the requisite holes were provided and the waste simply dropped down the shaft into the moat or ditch below. This would certainly have deterred any attacker from attempting to swim across!

At Chepstow Castle a two-hole garderobe survives today and was built suspended 200 feet above the River Wye. Garderobe shafts can also still be seen in Surrey at Guildford and Farnham Castles. At Guildford the shafts are very short and situated high up in the keep and most of the waste must have slithered down the outside wall before dropping into the castle ditch. Garderobes could be draughty places in which to defecate and they were certainly not the place to take the Sunday newsparchment!

[2]

The Gong Fermers

The best quality medieval houses would also have had their garderobes or privies and it is probable that it was about this time that the word 'privy' first came into use. A wealthy town merchant might have had several privies built into the walls of his house, just like the aristocracy up in the castle. The waste from the privies dropped down a shaft into a stone-lined pit, which was sometimes hidden in the cellar. The less wealthy or the slovenly simply allowed their muck to form a stinking pile against an outside wall. Examples of both would have existed in medieval towns like Guildford. How to dispose of this rotting heap of human excrement became something of a problem. Fortunately, by this time, a very specialist occupation, and a well paid one too, was beginning to become established. Someone took on the task of taking away that putrid heap or shovelling out the human dung from the pit. They usually worked at night.

The people with the unenviable task of wading into other people's muck were called 'rakers' or 'gong fermers' – gong or gang was another name for a privy, fermer comes from 'to fey', meaning 'to cleanse'. With scoops, shovels and buckets, strong stomachs and a poor sense of smell, the gong fermers removed the vile waste which was taken away and dumped onto the fields. Quite rightly they were well rewarded. In 1450 one household was charged 17s for 'ye caryyng a way of vi ton of dounge' and a further 5s 6d for 'dygyng of a pyt and takeyng owte of a serteyne of dounge owte of a privey and for to bery ye dounge in ye same pyt'.

The privy could be a dangerous place. As early as 1016 the King of Wessex, Edmund Ironside, was murdered whilst seated on his loo. His murderer 'awaytynge his tyme, espyed when the kynge was at the withdraught to purge nature, and with a spere strake hym into the foundement, and so into the body, whereof kyng Edmunde dyed shortly after'. A draught or withdraught was yet another name for a privy.

Privy pits could also be very deep and difficult to get out of should you have the misfortune to fall in. In 1326, a gong fermer called Richard the Raker, who should have known better, plunged through the rotten boards of his own privy and was found drowned in his own excrement. Perhaps he spent too much time looking after other people's arrangements to look after his own!

In the crowded medieval town the dumping of sewage in the streets and the emptying of 'pysse pottes' from upstairs windows was not as readily accepted as most of us have been led to believe. R. J. Mitchell and M. D. R. Leys, writing in *A History of London Life* about conditions in the capital in the medieval period, commented that 'if throwing out slops on to the heads of passers-by had been considered proper behavior it would not have excited rebuke; "Marjery", who was well-known also as a scold, was indicted less for her anti-social manners of speech than because "by the day and night [she] throws out of house her stinking ordure to the very great nuisance of her neighbours".' Whilst the courts attempted to curb the worst excesses, the authorities put the onus firmly on the townsfolk to remove all 'dirt and filth' from their streets. By the 14th century London had one latrine for each of the city wards, including one on London Bridge itself, which caused much annoyance to passing sailors and fishermen.

Through many centuries the Mayor of Guildford and his

A medieval straight-drop privy with a good pile of human manure beneath it. It was piles of 'dounge' like this which caused such problems for town authorities.

'Approved Men' watched vigilantly over the cleanliness of their borough. Any inhabitant guilty of leaving filth and waste in the streets could expect a stiff fine. In 1545 Richard Ace, Thomas Smallom and William Martyr, along with several others, were each fined 2d because they had permitted 'their very fetid and noisome gutters to run in the High Street to the common nuisance of the king's lieges'. A year later dozens more offenders were relieved of cash for leaving 'their dungheaps, very fetid and noisome to the king's lieges, in Le North Towne Dyche'. John Whelar and

Henry Nymes were also both fined 4d for causing 'fetid gutters to run in Le South Lane'. It was not the first time John Whelar had been fined for this offence.

By the late medieval period the rich and kingly had developed a liking for the close stool, later to become known as the commode. This device consisted of a box with a lid and a nicely padded seat with hole situated above a pot. The whole apparatus was often richly decorated and later versions were sometimes provided with armrests for greater comfort. King Henry VIII kept one in a little room situated just off the State Bedchamber called the Stool Room. The pot was emptied, no doubt down the nearest garderobe, by a man of great influence at Court, the Groom of the Stool, whose maintenance of his position must have depended upon whether His Majesty had succeeded in having 'a very fair siege'.

Henry had several palaces in Surrey – Oatlands, Nonsuch and Richmond, with Hampton Court nearby across the River Thames on the Middlesex bank. Both he and later his daughter, Elizabeth I, were constantly on the move from palace to palace, or making the most of the hospitality of the rich amongst their subjects. There was good sense in such a strategy as one contemporary observer wrote whilst staying in London during the reign of Elizabeth: 'The Queen has not been here since the 21st of June and does not return until October; she moves from one summer residence to another for change of air, it being very unhealthy here at this time of the year'. The state of the capital's sewers, including the River Thames, was a major contributor to the unhealthy conditions found in London, especially in summertime, and there was always the risk of the plague. Each year there came an exodus of the rich and royal as soon as the summer heat arrived.

Richmond Palace where the gong fermers employed by Elizabeth I were regularly kept busy. The gong fermers' livelihood was only momentarily threatened when she installed a flush loo here in about 1596. (Surrey Archaeological Society)

Not that Elizabeth stayed too long at any one time at her palaces in the clear air of Surrey and there was good reason for this too. The entourage of servants and hangers-on, who went everywhere with her, produced huge amounts of excrement. Very rapidly the 'houses of easement' or 'jakes', as they were called, became completely clogged and a certain unhealthy smell began to pervade the rooms and galleries. It was time to move on and leave the palace privies to the gong fermers. By the time she returned, perhaps months later, those unsung heroes had indeed made it a home fit for a queen once more.

An improvement seemed at hand when, in 1596, Sir John Harington, a godson of the Queen, invented a flushing water closet and he quietly installed the first fully working version in his house near Bath. However, he was encouraged by a friend to make his invention more widely known as it would

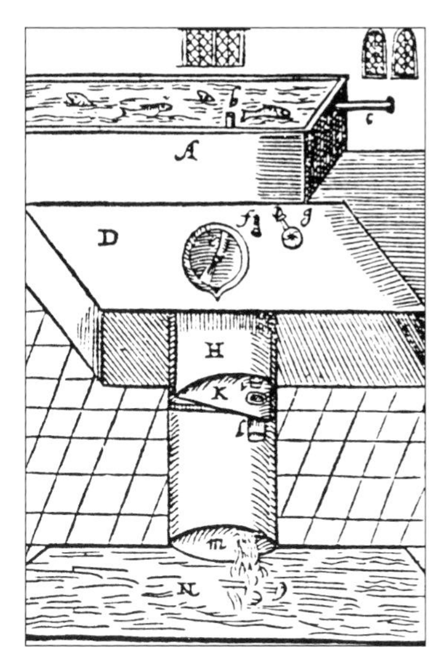

Sir John Harington's flush loo was installed at Richmond Palace. Perhaps I should read his book as it's not clear from this diagram exactly how it worked! (Surrey Archaeological Society)

'not only pleasure many great persons, but also do Her Majesty great service in her palace of Greenwich and other stately houses, that are oft annoyed with such savours as where many mouths are fed, can hardly be avoided'.

Harington's invention obviously made some impression on the Queen for she had one of his water closets installed in Richmond Palace. Sir John wrote a book entitled *The Metamorphosis of Ajax* (a play on the words 'a jakes', meaning a privy) and he prefaced the book with some verses including one 'to the Ladies of the Queen's Privy Chamber, at the making of their perfumed Privy at Richmond'. Unfortunately, his invention went no further and nearly 200 years passed before England was to see another flush loo.

[3]

A Winning Flush

Although, like a card player, the nobility of England may have wished for a good flush, it was a long time coming. In fact, during the 17th century the average Englishman's sanitary arrangements seem to have declined. Samuel Pepys visited the famous spa at Epsom in July 1663 to benefit from the laxative qualities of the water, but at the well he found no privies. Pepys drank two pots of the stuff, which had an instant effect, and he noted 'how everybody turns up his tail . . . in a bush'. He was back four years later for another dose of 'Epsom Salts' and 'did drink four pints, and had some very good stools by it'.

The origins of our preoccupation with 'keeping regular' are probably as old as homo sapiens himself. Prehistoric man must have known which plants would help with a successful evacuation of the bowels should he be overdue. The Romans certainly knew how to shift a lazy stool and medieval herbalists had many effective recipes. By Victorian times there was a plethora of laxatives to choose from – Boots Confection of Senna and Californian Syrup of Figs being, perhaps, the most popular.

'Syrup of Figs' continued to give success in the 'little room' well into the 20th century and I recall that a bottle of the stuff was an essential tool in an aunt's medicine cabinet. It was also the cause of some little misfortune for a group of German POWs held at a camp near Banstead. It was just after the Second World War, when sugar was in short supply, but the German cooks thought themselves lucky to discover a

Boots Confection of Senna provided relief for many a constipated Victorian. Hunyadi Janos Mineral Water, named after the famous medieval Hungarian hero, was described as 'the best aperient', aperient being a name for laxative medicine. (Roy Drysdale)

cache of bottles of 'Californian Syrup of Figs'. It tasted good and sweet so, not understanding its real purpose, they used it as a sugar substitute in their puddings. Apparently, for the next day or two the latrines at the camp were in great demand!

As well as 'Syrup of Figs' many will also remember those essentials to regularity, Beecham's Pills and Beecham's Powders. I am reminded of a terrible childhood rhyme:

> Down in the toilet ten feet deep
> There lies a sausage fast asleep.
> Do not wake him, do not dare,
> Beecham's pills have done their share!

Today, the shelves of our local chemist still groan under the weight of a huge choice of laxatives, proving that the matter is just as important to us as it was to our Victorian ancestors.

During the first half of the 18th century there may have been concoctions to assist the going, but where to go and how to get rid of it still taxed the scientific mind. The early part of the century saw the construction of several loos which made use of a flow of water, usually from a stream, to carry away the waste, just as the monks had done several centuries earlier. Queen Anne in the 1700s had 'a closet that leads to a little place of easement of marble with sluices of water to wash all down' installed at Windsor. Sir John Vanbrugh, architect of Blenheim Palace, built a magnificent stone loo for the owner of Hampden Manor in Oxfordshire, which relied on the flow provided by a drainage ditch. These loos, however, did not deliver a flush of water as and when it was required.

It was not until a watchmaker, Alexander Cummings, took out a patent for a valve-operated water closet in 1775 that relief was in sight. Cummings' system had an overhead cistern and a sliding valve operated by a pull-up handle but it

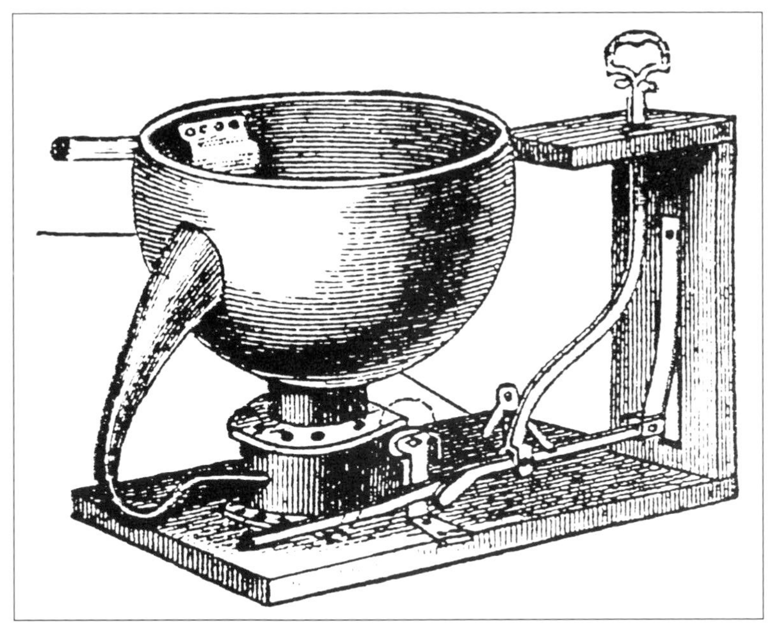

The mechanism of the 'Bramah' shown here would have been enclosed in a wooden case.

was unreliable. However, three years later Joseph Bramah, a cabinet maker, refined Cumming's invention, particularly the valve, and the first practical flush toilet had arrived. The Bramah soon became the fashionable as well as functional accessory in town house and country seat. Over 6,000 had been installed throughout Britain by 1797 and the word 'bramah' entered the English language as meaning something that was particularly good.

These new refinements were, of course, strictly for the well-off but in the towns, in particular, they simply shifted the problem to someone else. For the poorer inhabitants there was the bog house or privy, usually one per tenement for the lucky or one for a whole street for those at the bottom of the social ladder. The effluent from both privy and flush loo ran into cesspits, where it was sometimes left to soak away because the inhabitants cared little where their sewage went or because they were too poor to pay the night soil men to carry it away. Sometimes the foul smelling slurry crept under the floorboards and into cellars, or into the nearest well which was the main source of drinking water. Where there were drains the sewage usually found its way, untreated, into the nearest stream or river. At Southwark, which was part of Surrey until 1889, it was reported that human excrement was often piled up in the streets and then sold as manure.

The arrival of the dreaded disease of cholera into England in the 1830s finally, but painfully slowly, convinced Parliament that some action was needed. The Public Health Act of 1848 and several subsequent Acts empowered local authorities to look into the state of their towns and implement measures to alleviate the worst of the problem. The reports produced as a result make interesting reading!

At Guildford in 1849 it was revealed that most of the town's effluent went straight into the River Wey by the side of the Town Bridge at the bottom of the High Street. This was just upstream of a low-lying area occupied by many of the town's poor, who lived in cramped conditions in poor housing. Many were to die from cholera, the last recorded outbreak in Guildford being in 1866. Work did not start on a main sewerage system for the county town until 1889.

At Richmond it was reported in 1849 that 'there was no system of drainage, nearly all the houses were drained from cesspools, the earth was saturated with sewage, a large part of the water supply was obtained from shallow wells in the neighbourhood of the cesspools, and the general condition of the place, especially of the poorer dwellings, was most deplorable'.

At Epsom an inquiry was held which found a very similar

story. 'A large proportion of the houses in Epsom are badly built' and 'the privies are mostly wooden cabins . . . with cesspools. The closeness of these places to the houses coops up the air contained in them, and the foul stench finds its way into the buildings.' Local inhabitants were interviewed, including the daughter of James Hooper, who was forced to live next door to a large pile of pig manure. 'We have two rooms: one for living and one for sleeping. There is a hole through the wall, and a pigsty and a cowhouse built against the house. There is very often a bad smell in the house. We are obliged to carry all the slops and rubbish to the privy: we have nowhere else to put them . . .'

In the *Surrey Guardian* of July 1857 one correspondent decried the state of the sanitation of certain parts of Redhill: 'It is impossible to say we are not in any danger when we look at the state of Grove Place, so badly drained and so thickly inhabited; four families in one house; a man, his wife and five children in one small room; in another room in the same house, a man with five children, 13 persons in two small rooms, besides a family in each of the other rooms. The small yard at the back of the house is in a filthy state. Surely people who pay £18 per annum for their houses ought to have at least proper drainage . . .'

This situation was common to all Surrey towns and in some cases it was many years before any steps were taken to alleviate the problem. Reigate got off the mark soon after it became a borough in 1864 and began laying a proper drainage system. This was good news for the inhabitants of Redhill, which formed part of the new borough. By 1876 large sections of the borough including Reigate Town and Redhill had a sewerage system.

The Reigate Borough Sanitary Committee kept a watchful eye on those who still had an old fashioned privy, obliging house owners to change their habits when a sewer pipe had been provided. For example, in October 1880 the Committee resolved 'that the owner of premises in Bell Street, Reigate, occupied by Miss E. Taylor, be required to empty the boghole and fill it in with earth, to provide a closet pan and trap and connect the drainage with the sewer . . .' A year later they 'resolved that proceedings be taken against the owners of all houses at Reigate where nuisances exist caused by defective privies'.

Once in the pipe Reigate's sewage flowed along to the outfall at the sewage farm at Earlswood, where it was disposed of by 'the system of broad irrigation', meaning the liquid matter was simply allowed to soak away and the rest then ploughed into the ground.

Meanwhile, the situation in most Surrey villages was still poor. At Newdigate in 1900 it was reported that a tiny two-bedroomed cottage was occupied by a family of eight. In one bedroom slept Henry Burrows with his wife and three of their children. Three further children slept in the other bedroom, where the ceiling was open to the thatched roof. Downstairs there was a stone-paved living room and a washhouse. The outside toilet arrangements consisted simply of a seat protected by a wooden roof on four poles. There were no drains.

Whilst some Surrey towns had begun to make improvements by the 1880s, others lagged behind. At Sutton in 1898 the Medical Officer of Health reported that there was contamination of wells due to seepage through the chalk from cesspools; 181 premises were said to be affected. In 1893 Woking was described as a town where 'there was no drainage, no lighting and no made roads except the main roads, the other so-called roads being mostly mere tracks often used as a convenient spot to deposit the contents of cesspools'. It was clearly time for all of Surrey to clean up its act!

[4]

Messrs Doulton, Crapper, Twyford And Shanks

The arrival of proper drainage systems in towns throughout Britain was a great spur to those entrepreneurs intent on making fortunes from the public's growing desire for comfort in the closet. Those men whose names are now synonymous with the modern bathroom, such as John Shanks, Thomas Twyford and Henry Doulton, introduced a huge range of lavatory pans often highly decorated with swirls of flowers or willow pattern. They gave their creations evocative names such as The Cymplur, Lambeth, Combination, Excelsior, Perfecta, Clencher or The Ripple, Revolver or Rocket!

'The Royal' still in daily use in Warlingham. (Len Blackmore)

Henry Doulton, whose main potteries were at Lambeth, which was part of Surrey until 1889, played a very important part in the development of the modern loo and was knighted for his efforts. He also had his country seat (well, several of them!) in Surrey at Ewhurst. Here at Rapsley he laid experimental stoneware drainage pipes, which were made in his factory, and he also invented a stoneware trap to prevent sewage gases from finding their way back into the closet. Sir Henry had a new house, Woolpits, built in 1885 not far from Rapsley and here he installed all the latest lavatorial technology straight from his works. I was fortunate to be invited to inspect his private bathroom at Woolpits, now the Duke of Kent School, thanks to the headmaster, Mr Wilson. I was shown to the room by Di Day, the school secretary, where I found a dazzling display of blue and brown bathroom tiles and the arched alcove to take his bath. Unfortunately, no

Instructions on how to use Doulton's Patent Syphon Flushing Cistern. (Len Blackmore)

other original features had survived from Sir Henry Doulton's reign on this particular throne.

There was, of course, one other pioneer of the flush loo who must not be forgotten. The plumbing successes of Thomas Crapper added a new word to the English language, which was first recorded in that capacity, according to my dictionary, in 1898. From humble beginnings in Yorkshire, Crapper established a company based in Chelsea which was eventually supplying toilets, sinks and baths to royalty. He greatly improved the toilet cistern and soon the 'Crapper Valveless Waste Preventer' was being installed in all the best houses.

I visited a fine house in Ewhurst belonging to Barry Morgan, which was built in the 1900s. The bathroom had once been entirely kitted out by Crapper's company. Unfortunately, the cisterns and toilet bowls had been replaced but 'T. Crapper & Co Ltd, Chelsea' was still firmly imprinted upon the tops of the wash basin taps and Crapper's initials were on the basins themselves.

Like Henry Doulton, Thomas Crapper wrestled with the problems caused when sewer gases escaped into the house. Apart from the evil smell the gases produced, they were also poisonous and highly explosive. Violent combustions in the lavatory often took on a much more literal meaning! Crapper came up with the U bend, a device now found in every bathroom and toilet, and one very much taken for granted, and the problem was solved.

Thomas Crapper also developed the 'trough closet' for use in factories, institutions and workhouses. These closets consisted of a row of toilets with a common channel running underneath, which flushed automatically when full. The trough closet was very successful and some survived until quite recently. However, there was, as a Farncombe resident

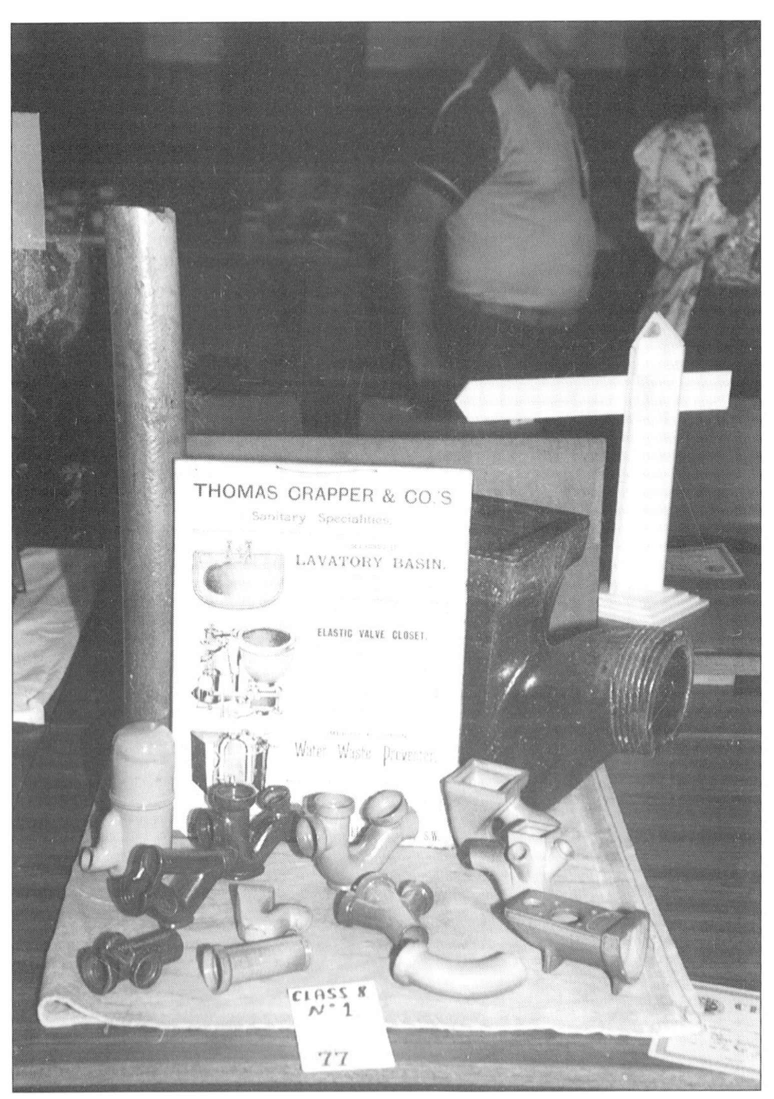

A prize winning display of Thomas Crapper samples seen at a bottle collectors' show. (Len Blackmore)

Chain pull handles were manufactured for local Surrey companies – on the right for George Cummins & Son of Dorking. (Len Blackmore)

related to me, one particular disadvantage if you had the misfortune to be seated above the 'downstream' end of the channel. It was not unknown for the cruel and mischievous to drop lighted paper boats down into the channel, where they floated off until meeting a pocket of recently introduced gas. The resultant explosion caused more than just a loud bang!

The facilities provided, thanks to the fertile minds of the likes of Thomas Crapper and Henry Doulton, solved a delicate problem for the rich and fashionable. They also provided comfort for the 'towny' once the drains had been laid. But what of those rural corners of Surrey? I wrote letters to the local newspapers and asked whether their readers had any memories of this more private side of life. The response was tremendous.

Inside a Surrey privy. (Roy Drysdale)

I found that out in the country many of Surrey's inhabitants had to resort to the dubious pleasure of using the 'privy', when the rest of us had long taken the flush for granted. I learnt that the Surrey privy was usually a tiny wooden or tin shack, often situated some distance down the garden path from the user's cottage home. More luxurious privies were built in brick or stone and some even had a small window to provide a little light to daytime visitors. For groups of cottages privies were often built in pairs, side by side or back to back, or in blocks, which made going to the loo a very sociable affair. Inside the privy there was a flat wooden board with the appropriate hole, where the user's bottom hovered above an abyss. A night visit was only for the desperate when, clutching a guttering candle or oil lamp, they made their faltering way towards the blackness, the spiders and the bogeymen!

It was clear from my desktop investigations that the general use of privies in the rural parts of Surrey had continued well into the 20th century. Even as late as the 1960s a surprising number were still in use and there are parts of the county which still have no mains drainage. But had any of these unobtrusive little buildings, once essential to the everyday lives of so many Surrey people, survived? The privy surely represented an aspect of the county's social history which must receive more than a footnote before passing from remembered history. Any surviving privies needed recording and photographing, surviving memories put to paper. Friends were sceptical, their worries about my sanity perhaps confirmed, but I sensed the fun of a chase. It was time to leave my desk and get out and search.

[5]

A Privy Quest

'It's over there somewhere,' said my guide, Hugo Russell. 'It's not been used for a long time, not since the old cottages were demolished and the new house built.'

I was at Farley Green near Albury and armed with secateurs and a stout pair of old boots. My quest for the elusive Surrey privy had entered a new phase. Through the rampant and very prickly undergrowth I gradually snipped my way towards a wooden door, half hidden behind the slope of a heavily leaning birch tree.

Eventually, after what seemed to be an extraordinarily long time, I was at the door, its brown paint peeling off in slivers. With bleeding hand (I had left the gardening gloves at home) I made to push the door open. But, with hand on the door, I suddenly hesitated. 'Should I knock before going in?' I pondered. After all, it would have been the polite thing to do. I tapped twice and then gently swung the door back. And there it was! The wooden seat intact and down the hole I could see that the privy bucket was still in position, waiting for a caller who never came. There was a little hinged door at the front below the seat, kept in place with a metal catch, to enable the bucket to be extracted for emptying. A long frond of ivy growing through the wooden back wall was draped artistically across the seat.

'Where exactly were the old cottages?' I asked Hugo, as I extricated myself from the undergrowth.

'Exactly where the modern house is now,' he replied. 'There were two cottages but they were in a terrible

Messrs Hugo Russell and Son, privy hunters – the tiled roof of a privy can be seen deep in the undergrowth behind the right-hand shed. (Roy Drysdale)

condition and were condemned,' he continued. I noted that the distance from cottage to privy must have been a good 30 yards at least. I was already beginning to learn something about the problems of visiting the loo in times past.

'Was there just one privy for both cottages?' I asked.

'Oh no, they had one each. There's another privy in there somewhere, on the other side of the shed,' he replied.

Eventually I found the second privy, but time had not been kind to this relic. It was built entirely of overlapping wooden planks like a garden shed. The collapsed corrugated iron roof had been pushed down inside the building. It was obvious that any attempt to get inside would probably lead to the entire structure teetering over to become a heap of unrecognisable rubbish. After a quick reconnoitre, it was left in peace.

Inside the privy at Farley Green. (Roy Drysdale)

I knew before I started the hunt that there were several different types of privy. This trip to Farley Green had introduced me to what was to prove to be by far the most common type I was to find in Surrey – the bucket privy. There were then two basic versions of the bucket privy. The bucket was removed for emptying either via a small door beneath the front of the seat or from the outside through a flap usually provided at the base of the back wall.

Bucket privies usually had only one hole, which could be dangerous for younger children who sometimes fell in! Privies with cesspits could be much more sophisticated in hole provision – some had two holes including one of small dimensions, often with a step, for the younger members of the family. Three-holers and even four-holers were not unknown so several members of the family could sit down together.

Some cottages in Pirbright had movable privies. A hole was dug in the garden and the privy, a simple wooden shed, was balanced over the hole. After a while (sometimes months!), when the hole was full or had become too 'pongy', a new hole was dug elsewhere in the garden, the privy repositioned and the old hole capped with some of the freshly dug soil. One of the problems, I was told, especially in a small garden was finding a 'fresh' patch of garden.

'We used to have a bucket of ashes from the fire on the floor in the dunny as we called it and, after you'd been, you had to sprinkle some ashes down the hole to cover what you'd done. The dry ashes seemed to kill off a lot of the pong,' a neighbour told me, having read about my latest interest in the local newspaper.

Marie Kite of Pirbright told me about her initial experience of using a privy: 'My first memory of an outside toilet situated some distance from the house was in 1940 when I met a young soldier at Aylesbury, who lived at Pirbright. The soldier was later to become my husband. He had a week's leave and took me home to meet his family. They lived in a lovely old bungalow with a beautiful garden, well off the village in the woods. There was no electricity, the bungalow was lit with oil lamps, and the toilet was about 25 yards from the house. There was a box and a shovel in the corner with the ash from the fire, which you threw into the bucket after use.'

The weather-boarded privy that Mr Trower remembered as a child was constructed above a cesspit. 'At the old family home we had at Peaslake,' wrote Mr Trower, 'a box of lime and a box of sifted ashes were kept inside our loo with a small hand shovel and after using the loo you put a small shovelful of each down the hole.'

This use of ashes reminded me of a privy invention by the

A Godalming privy survives amongst the ivy and builder's rubble. (Roy Drysdale)

Reverend Henry Moule, who in 1860 patented an earth closet which, at the pull of a handle, delivered a measured portion of dry earth or ashes into the privy bucket. The operation of the handle was either 'pull out' or 'pull up', but there was also the 'self-acting' version which operated automatically as soon as the user rose from the seat. The redoubtable cleric also developed a portable version which might have been useful for early caravanners! Moule's earth closets were extremely popular and could still be purchased in the 1930s.

It was all a matter of keeping it dry that made the difference between a stinking privy and a comfortable and wholesome 'place of easement'. Because of this it was taboo in many privies for the males of the household to use it simply to have a wee. Mary Gatford of Chilworth remembers the chamber pots provided for both sexes in her grandparents' privy.

'To save having to empty the bucket too often, most men just urinated outside on the back wall of the privy. This had been going on so long that they had worn quite a large hole in the board wall!' wrote Mr A. J. Cunningham about a friend's privy in Ewhurst in the late 1940s.

For a really dry privy let us now turn to Charles Richardson who, in 1886, published his specification for a 'dry privy, minimum size, for a cottage':

> Built with 9in brick walls, and brick on edge flooring, 4ft 6in by 3ft in the clear. It will take 4 cubic yards of brickwork and may be built for about £5.
>
> A dry privy may also be safely built as a lean-to against

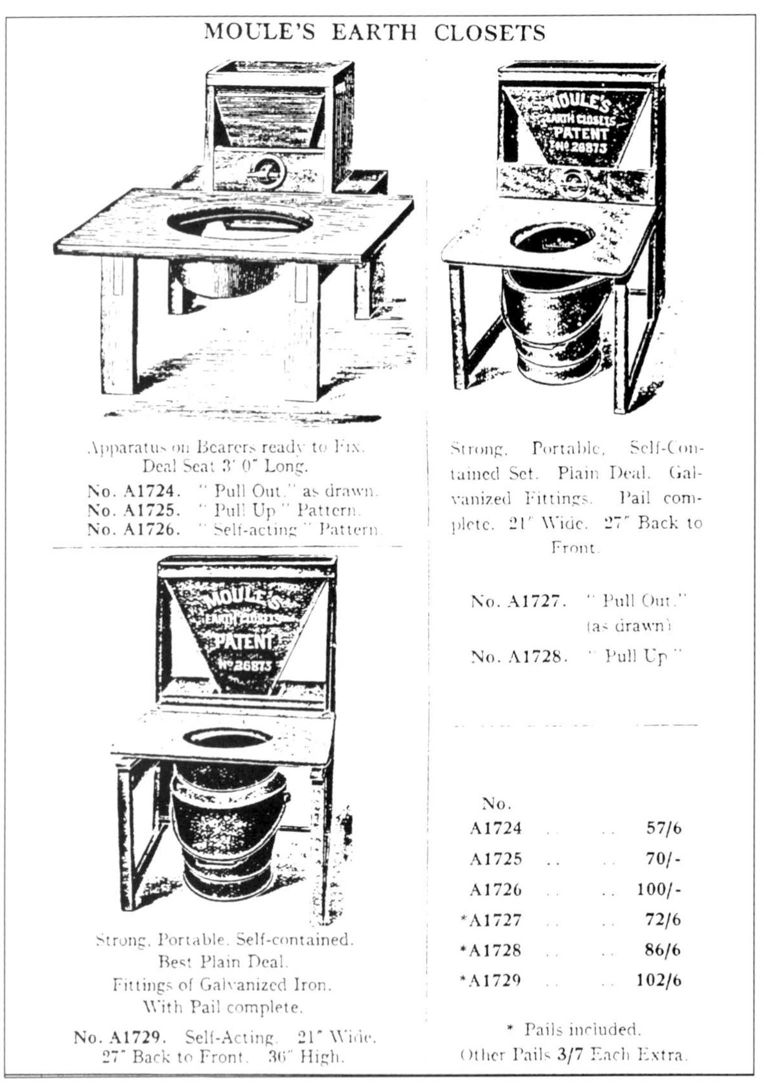

Although the Rev Henry Moule's earth closet was invented in 1860, it was still available in 1936, the date of this advert from an ironmonger's catalogue.

the back wall of a cottage, by which means the cost of the front wall will be saved. The door will then be on the side. The back should, in all cases, join the garden bed.

It must always be borne in mind that the essential features of the dry privy are: firstly, that the droppings should be kept DRY, and secondly, that they should be kept ABOVE the surface soil.

For this purpose the floor of the privy is raised two steps above the ground level, in order to form a 'catch' behind at ground level; the floor of this catch should slope slightly outwards, so that any moisture should naturally drain that way into a small heap of earth which has been tipped against that archway at the back.

The result of this arrangement is, that we are coming back to Nature, who has provided the surface soil to catch and purify things. We thus avoid entirely the formation of sewage, and the consequent pollution of our wells, water-springs and rivers, and the propagation of fevers and zymotic diseases in general.

The dry privy requires no looking after, and is never offensive; all that it requires is that it should be emptied once every six months or so, and this is done without trouble in five minutes, when the earth and the droppings are shovelled out on the level and mixed with a little more earth, after which a barrow full of fresh earth is tipped against the archway, and that is all that is wanted. If what has been taken out is left in a heap for two or three weeks it becomes valuable manure for the garden.

Old-fashioned privies, instead of having the floor raised two steps above the surface, in order to form a 'catch' usually have cesspits dug into the ground; these are a mistake, for they hold water, and thus form sewage, which makes a privy offensive and sometimes the cause of propa-

> gation of fevers around them; besides making the emptying of them a very difficult and offensive operation.

Would I find examples of the dry privy as recommended by Charles Richardson during my researches in Surrey? The answer came when I visited Peter Gellatly at his farmhouse south of Shere. The privy was solidly constructed of local stone with brick quoins and the mortared joints had been 'galleted' by pressing small pieces of ironstone into the mortar whilst it was still wet. It had a small window and was built into a steep bank behind the house. Although it had a door, of course, further privacy was provided by the fact that it was hidden behind the trunk of a large and venerable yew tree. Unfortunately, there was no roof.

'I'm afraid a large branch from the yew crashed through the roof during the Great Storm in 1987,' said Mr Gellatly. 'I'm hoping sometime to restore it.'

Inside, the privy had plastered walls and had last been painted in a tasteful shade of pale blue. It was full of slimy baulks of timber that had originally formed the main structure of the roof. Very carefully I removed the timbers and found the original seat but the elements had not been kind to this particular privy. The seat was so rotten that, had an ant in need tried to sit down on it, then it would surely have collapsed the entire structure! I removed the final lengths of timber, which were leaning in the corner, to find a globe-shaped glass jar, which would have contained the candle, still sitting in the corner having survived storm and tempest that violent night in October '87.

Mr Gellatly's privy looked on initial inspection to have been built as a bucket privy because there was the small door below the seat, but in this case collapsed underneath it. However, outside I noticed a sheet of corrugated iron

Inside Peter Gellatly's privy near Shere I found the glass jar for the candle still in position in the corner of the seat. (Roy Drysdale)

wedged against the side wall and half buried in the grassy bank. Could this hide an archway for a dry privy as described so well by Charles Richardson? The archway would have to be in the side wall as the back wall was almost buried in the bank.

Soon Mr Gellatly and I were enthusiastically shovelling earth. Eventually we managed to prise back the sheet of iron and exposed the top of an archway just as I had suspected. The privy had clearly been built as a dry privy but ended its working life as a simple bucket privy. When I left, Mr Gellatly seemed very keen on carrying out the restoration of his privy and I sincerely hope that he succeeds in doing so. The surviving privies of Surrey need all the help they can get.

The author looks on as Peter Gellatly digs into the bank in the hope of finding the arch of a dry privy behind the sheet of corrugated iron. (Roy Drysdale)

The remains of the arch revealed behind the corrugated iron sheet on the side wall of Peter Gellatly's privy near Shere. (Roy Drysdale)

[6]

Down The Garden Path

The privy could be a smelly place, so mostly it was sited as far away from the house or cottage as possible. Thus those wishing to go were often required to embark on a hazardous journey in order to reach relief, especially at night. At Hambledon I was shown a pair of privies where some skill in mountaineering might have been useful! After leaving the cottage the desperate privy seeker firstly had to climb a steep flight of steps, then carry on up a one in three incline before turning left and going about 40 yards across a sloping garden to the top of the hill. From the privy door, the expedition successfully completed, the intrepid mountaineer could now look down upon the roof of their home!

June Spong of Dorking wrote to me about her fond memories of trips to one particular privy: 'George, my future husband, lived in Gadbrook Farm House. It was an old rambling building with the "dunny" at the bottom of the garden. We would sit in the inglenook fireplace and "spoon" (well it was the 1950s) and drink homemade lemonade and beer. Soon, I would need to "take a walk in the garden". George would walk me through the flower beds, past the cabbages, over a little bridge that crossed a stream to a blue painted "outhouse". "Don't shut the door," I would cry. "Don't shut me in!"

'George would have to stand with his back to me so that I could see the light of his torch. Panic would set in if he made a move towards the house, which had no electricity and was lit by oil lamps.'

A pair of hill-top back-to-back brick privies at Hambledon. (Roy Drysdale)

Although Miss Riddle of Park Barn, Guildford, was lucky enough to have a flush toilet at her childhood home, reaching it was still quite an expedition: 'We lived in a row of houses up "The Mount" in Guildford, and our lavatories were situated in a row at the end of a concrete passage. As our house was in the middle of the block, we had to go past three houses to get to them. It was scary going down there after dark and I remember I always wanted my sister to come down with me. We were lucky in that we had a flush cistern, but being outside meant it always froze up in the colder winters we seemed to have then. So for weeks at a time we had to cart buckets of water down with us.'

Mrs Hubbard of Witley remembered her childhood privy: 'We did indeed have a chilly walk in those days, down the garden to the privy armed not only with an oil lamp but also a bucket of water for flushing. It was quite a long walk and consequently one usually had a wet foot, on the bucket side, by the time of arrival from the same bucket over-spilling on the journey.'

'I was brought to live in Haslemere at the age of six. I can remember we actually had to walk out of a gate and up a little hill to our privy,' said Audrey Creasey. 'But the privy I remember most was at my grandmother's in the countryside nearby. We had to walk about 25 yards to the little wooden shed with a candle in a jam jar in winter.'

Mrs Bache of Guildford spent her childhood on a farm at Worplesdon and she well remembered the long walk to the privy. 'We had to go along a long path to the wood, cum coal, cum everything–else shed to go to the loo. There was a tiny part of the shed partitioned off, complete with door.'

This pair of back-to-back brick privies are situated a long walk down the garden path at Ewhurst. (Roy Drysdale)

The privy rarely had a lock or bolt on the door, so singing loudly was often the only way of letting others know that it was occupied. A length of string would be attached to the door. Once enthroned you held on to the string so the door could be kept open a little to allow some fresh air to get in. Pull the string and the door quickly shut without the occupier having to get off the seat when someone else approached. Mrs Hubbard remembers that they had a flagpole outside the door and the Union Jack would be raised to warn others that the privy was occupied and that the long trek down the garden would be in vain.

The privy was often hidden amongst the trees or surrounded by bushes to keep it from sight. As a child Mary Gatford of Chilworth had to wind her way through an orchard to reach the privy. A 'rather horrible place' is how she described it. As I mentioned in the previous chapter, Peter Gellatly's privy near Shere was secreted behind a yew tree. But it was very behind – the door to the privy being only about two feet from the tree's massive trunk.

'Our privy was not the best place for those with a delicate nose but it was surrounded by lilac trees and, for about a week or so just once a year, it was filled with a much more pleasant perfume!' one ex-resident of Dunsfold told me. Lilac seems to have been popular as a means of obscuring your privy. 'My grandfather's privy, which we called "the little house", was at the bottom of the garden and surrounded by lilac,' recalled Mary Gatford.

'Our loo [at Peaslake] was at the top of the garden under a plum tree,' my neighbour told me. And Miss Jordan recalled the privy at the family home in Redhill in the 1920s: 'Our closet was across a small cobbled yard. It was built onto the

A pair of 'side by side' brick privies separated by a garden wall at Mayford near Woking. (Roy Drysdale)

back of the coal shed and protected on the side by a full-grown thick yew hedge, some nine and a half feet tall and about five feet in length, shutting off the garden. It was also back-to-back with the neighbours' closet, they having the benefit of a large white cherry tree to screen the buildings. On the roof of our lav grew a magnificent house leek – very appropriate!'

To reach the privy at another childhood home near Redhill meant that Miss Jordan had to walk to 'the bottom of a long garden, not good on a dark, wet night in winter, but at least we had a torch by then. Much better than juggling with a candlestick, with one hand shielding the flame, the other one pushing away wet shrubs. One thing, as children we never stayed long in the "dunny" – my father's name for it.'

Many people, of course, managed to avoid the long trek to the privy at night by keeping a chamber pot beneath the bed. The 'gazunder' has a long history and I'm sure the Romans used pots for that purpose. They were certainly very popular by Tudor and Stuart times. At Guildford Museum I was shown some fine examples excavated from a pit in Tunsgate and dated to the late 17th century. That popular local, The Merry Harriers, at Hambledon has dozens of gazunders hanging from the ceiling beams in the bar. The landlord, Colin Beasley, told me that the collection started when a regular found an old chamber pot in the hedge on his way to the pub. After the pot had been used for beer instead of the usual tankard, it became the nucleus of a huge collection, which now takes hours to clean!

Hugo Russell of Shere was once the owner of a rather fine chamber pot, which was still occasionally used. Then some

Two late 17th century chamber pots found in a rubbish pit at Tunsgate, Guildford. (Roy Drysdale)

American visitors took a shine to it and were given it as a farewell present. When Hugo visited the gazunder's new owners in the United States and sat down for a meal, the chamber pot appeared on the table as a salad container. Hugo remembered its previous use and found it very difficult to eat the salad!

Even in the post-war period not everyone could boast of having access to a 'little house' or 'dunny' both at home and at work. Anthony Cunningham described to me the 'arrangements' he discovered when he started work at a garage on the Surrey/Hampshire border in 1951. 'The "boss" had a

Colin Beasley, landlord of The Merry Harriers at Hambledon, proudly displays a couple of fine gazunders from his large collection. (Roy Drysdale)

Gazunders make useful plant pots – the author dug the large chamber pot from a Victorian rubbish dump. (Roy Drysdale)

toilet in his house, adjoining the garage,' wrote Mr Cunningham, 'which was connected to a soak-away in the garden, but the staff were banned totally from using it with the exception of the office girl. If we needed a "pee" we had to go into a dark corner at the far end of the garage behind the coke heap, where there was an old, battered, toilet-type bucket standing on the floor. It had a metal pipe connected to the bottom of it leading to the garden through a hole in the wall. The smell was so disgusting that everyone used the coke heap, this in turn made a pretty awful smell when the coke was burnt in our school-type stove in the workshop!'

'Of course, if we needed a toilet for something more, continued Mr Cunningham, 'we had to walk 200 hundred yards down the main road in the village to the public house, clutching a newspaper etc and an "old" penny, or run if you were really desperate! You had to hope that the toilet was not occupied or too disgusting to use!'

Relief came to the male staff at the garage when a new boss took over two years after Anthony Cunningham had started work there. 'He said that we must have a "proper" toilet, so we built one out of wood in the opposite corner of the garage.' But there was to be no luxury of the flush toilet first perfected by Joseph Bramah in 1778. After all, this was only 1953, and a bucket privy is what they got!

[7]

Going Inside

When Audrey Monk of Hambledon heard that I was searching for privies she quickly volunteered to take me on a tour around her village. 'There are plenty of privies surviving here and one was still being used in 1994,' she enthused. 'You can't write a book on Surrey's privies without visiting here!'

So I set off for the village on a bright but cold late winter's morning, armed with all the equipment that an experienced privy hunter should carry or wear – stout boots, a warm but old jacket, trousers you might go fishing in, gardening gloves, camera, secateurs and a wallet.

When I first ventured out on my search for privies I found the prospect a little daunting. I worried a little about the reaction I might get when asking complete strangers if they had an old privy hidden in their garden. I thought of the curt or rude replies I was bound to get. I saw in my mind's eye large black dogs snapping at my heels as I rapidly retreated from the cries of 'get off my land!'

I had no need to worry. Everywhere I met friendly and chatty people, who were only too pleased to show me their privy or tell me about their experiences of using the 'little house at the end of the garden'. And on this particular morning, when I arrived at Audrey Monk's cottage in Hambledon, I found that she had already organised most of the introductions for me. Firstly, we visited Margaret and Gerald Jarvis, who had a nice brick-built privy which was back-to-back with an identical privy next door.

This privy in Hambledon is now used as a shed. Like several other privies I discovered, it also provides support for a nest box. (Roy Drysdale)

'Are there any original features inside?' I enquired hopefully.

'No, sorry, we use it as a shed,' Margaret replied.

I had already noted that the change of use from 'place of easement' to 'place of storage' had at least resulted in the survival of many more privy buildings than might otherwise have been the case. The inability of many of us to throw anything away 'because it might prove useful' has become an act of conservation in more ways than one. Next door to the Jarvis's cottage the story was similar, but this time the door had been removed and the privy now functioned as a wood store.

We then visited Joan Hardy next door to the village shop. Here we were warmly greeted by Joan and a very friendly visiting canine that Joan was looking after for friends. He took a great interest in our every move but his approach to the problem was akin to that of our prehistoric ancestors! Joan had a ramshackle wooden privy joined on to the back of the building but, again, inside it was bereft of original features. At the home of Mr and Mrs Hubsch down the road the wooden privy building had been carefully retained but its concrete floor supported nothing you could sit on.

At the next stop I needed to do some asking and the dogs sounded distinctly unfriendly as the owner pushed open a kitchen window to speak to me. But this was the cottage that had been the home of Rose Sage, who had died aged 104 in 1996. She had used her privy almost to the end and, when I pushed open the door of the stoutly constructed brick building in the corner of the garden, everything was just as she had left it. There was even a plastic bottle of loo cleaner in the corner of the seat and, for modern comfort, the wooden seat itself had also been provided with an additional plastic seat. The bucket below was also modern. I did not sit

This privy had been used until about 1994 by centenarian, Rose Sage. I opened the door to find her bottle of loo cleaner exactly where she had left it in the corner of the seat. (Roy Drysdale)

down, but standing in there it was easy to imagine Rose traversing her garden, heading towards her loo on a cold winter's morning. I felt that she would not have appreciated finding a complete stranger inside, so I quickly came out.

At the next cottage I spotted a privy of almost identical build to Rose Sage's, including a small window above the door. It was in good condition apart from a hole in the bottom of the door. We were kindly invited to view it by the owner, Fiona Greenhalgh. Again I asked the same now familiar question.

'Are there still any original bits inside?' I enquired, being keen to find another working privy.

'No, I don't think there's a seat or anything like that in there,' she answered. 'It's always been used as a store for firewood since we've lived here, but you're welcome to remove some of the wood just in case.'

Ten minutes of log shifting and a complete wooden seat with a single hole and privy bucket below was the reward. I carefully removed the bucket via the little door beneath the seat for a closer look. The gnawed hole at the bottom of the privy door was now explained. The bucket was full of acorns, some half chewed, the legacy of some thrifty squirrel (see photo page 67).

At Hambledon the National Trust owns Oakhurst Cottage, which has been locked in a time warp of two or three generations ago. The privy was a revelation – whitewashed inside, complete with mirror on the wall and the wooden box for the squares of newspaper. The privy bucket was still in position under the wooden seat and, on the edge of the seat, someone had placed a book. This place gave life to the many descriptions that people had given me of the inside of their privies.

Fiona Greenhalgh's privy cum woodstore at Hambledon. All the works were revealed underneath the logs, including the bucket. (Roy Drysdale)

'Our privy had a scrubbed wooden box with a hole cut in it, where a galvanised bucket was housed. On the left of the hole was a wooden box with neat sizes of newspaper in,' wrote one of my correspondents.

Mary Gatford's grandfather had a privy with 'an ivy covered roof and a blue door with decorated ventilation holes.' It was not unusual for the privy seat to have more than one hole and Mary described her grandfather's privy as having 'three holes in the wooden seat – an adult-sized hole at each end and a small one for children in the middle. Not content with just an ordinary plain seat, grandfather had decorated the seat with flowing carvings of leaves and vines.'

Mrs Bache recalled that on the family farm at Worplesdon

The visitor to the privy at Oakhurst Cottage has been thoughtfully provided with some reading matter. (Roy Drysdale)

'the toilet itself comprised two wooden seats – one for adults and a lower one with a smaller hole for children'. Mr Trower of Farley Green also remembered a similar arrangement for the two-holer at his childhood home in Peaslake. There were also three and even four-holers but these seem to have been rare in Surrey. The seat for a four-holer rescued from Tilford is preserved in the Old Kiln Museum nearby.

Mary Gatford also mentioned to me that her 'grandmother was very house-proud and kept the privy beautifully clean. The walls were regularly whitewashed and even the brick floor was painted red. Grandfather put panels of wood at the back of the seats so that people could lean back in luxury.'

Like Mary's grandmother many owners tried to keep their privies scrupulously clean and the seat was regularly scrubbed. 'Our privy or "funny place", as I called it, had a large wooden seat, like all others in existence it went from one side wall to the other. As the only girl I had the task of scrubbing the seat with hot water and carbolic soap,' wrote Miss Jordan of the privy she knew as a child in Redhill. 'I had to do this every Saturday morning, along with other chores.'

The good privy owner usually whitewashed the inside once a year and, if the building itself was wooden, it might also get a coat of tar or creosote on the outside.

'The walls were given a fresh coat of whitewash every spring,' continued Miss Jordan, 'and with three brothers to help we wrote, in pencil, short lines or drew pictures on the finished white surface. My father never complained. About 1934 the walls became a delicate shade of pink and we gave up our writing.'

White was clearly the favourite for internal decoration in the privy, followed by pink, but during my privy hunt I also

The seat for a four-holer has been preserved at the Old Kiln Museum at Tilford. (Chris Shepheard/Farnham Buildings Preservation Trust)

came across pale blue, green, yellow and a revolting shade of purple. With carved, decorated seats and even wallpaper, it was amazing what some owners would do to make their privy as comfortable as their home!

[8]

Here Comes The Lavender Van

Mr and Mrs Taylor of Hambledon remember the weekly visits of the night soil men. Their aunt's privy still survives up the end of a very steep back garden and every Wednesday the bucket had to be carried down the garden. Great care was needed to avoid the horrors of a tidal wave in the bucket causing an overflow down the leg. The bucket was then parked on the garden wall by the road ready for the visit of the 'lavender men'. These heroes emptied the contents into their 'lavender van', cleaned out and disinfected the bucket and returned it to the wall. Hambledon's last lavender man emptied his last bucket in about 1994 and with him died a craft whose lineage stretched back to the gong fermers of medieval England.

The lavender van or honey cart, as it was also euphemistically called, had become a feature of most of Surrey's towns long before the particular skills of those who rode the carts had reached the county's rural villages. However, the system had certain teething problems in the early days. Carts which were unsuitable and 'night soil' collected during the day were chief amongst complaints received by the authorities.

For example, by 1875 much of Farnham Town had switched to bucket privies. In that year George Trimmer, a leading local brewer, complained of 'the filthy practice of the Night Soil Men removing the contents of Privies in Carts unfit for the purpose'. Ewbank Smith in his book, *Victorian Farnham*, suggested that 'these carts worked very much on

'Nightmen' as depicted in Henry Mayhew's 'London Labour and the London Poor' published in 1861.

the same principle as a cat's dirtbox, only larger'. Mr Trimmer reported that he had seen carts in Guildford made especially for the purpose and advocated the purchase of one. Eventually one was purchased and hired out to the night soil men at 1s a load. The need for the cart and the services of the men ended when Farnham acquired a mains drainage system during the 1880s.

At Leatherhead the authorities saw no reason to go to all the expense of proper sewers and opted instead for the 'Rochdale Pail dry closet system'. In March 1881 an initial 150 pails with lids were ordered for the good folk of the town and one Henry Jewell engaged to empty them.

This privy bucket had been used as an acorn store by a thrifty squirrel. (Roy Drysdale)

The contents of the 'Rochdale Pails' were collected by cart and then taken to fields adjacent to the town, and ploughed into the ground. The authorities were so satisfied with the system that the inspector appointed by the Parochial Committee to oversee it, Mr Mather, was awarded a gratuity of £5. But all was not running as smoothly as they believed and a letter was received from a local resident, Mr Still, who wrote that 'a large number of ratepayers were strongly opposed to the present system of drainage and were anxious that some alteration should be made. The carts collected the sewage about the streets at all times of the day, causing a very great nuisance . . . Surely it could be arranged that the carts should be about the streets either late at night or early in the morning?'

In a letter to the local paper in October 1891 a Mr Cunliffe complained about the daytime activities of the privy carts in Leatherhead and wrote that 'recently my daughter was driving through the town, when she had to pass one of the carts, and the smell was most sickening . . .' Mr Cunliffe referred to the fact that the night soil (or should it have been 'day soil'?) was deposited near to the High Road and he demanded that 'the work of collecting and disposing of it might be carried out without causing so great a nuisance.' The clerk of the Parochial Committee replied that the collection of the town's night soil now took place 'in the forenoon instead of at all times of the day as previously' and that 'the pail system had proved to be an immense boon to the many occupiers of small property, and that since the adoption of the system the general health [of Leatherhead] had greatly improved'. The Committee decided to take no action and it was well into the 1900s before the town's 'Rochdale Pail' system was to disappear.

In *A Century of Village Memories*, Judy Parfitt recorded the memories of Douglas David, who was born at Mogador, Lower Kingswood near Banstead in 1924: 'Mr Chalcraft . . . had a horse and cart which was used to collect the buckets from the houses, as of course no sewerage was laid on. A clean bucket, dusted with disinfectant powder, was exchanged for the full one. This raw sewage was then emptied onto Rookery Farm fields and covered with straw. When many of the houses were given cesspools, the tanker lorry would drive round this field trailing its pipe and allowing the sewage to cover the land!'

Out in other rural parts of the county, the authorities took a long time before providing a bucket emptying service. I found a newspaper report from 1921 concerning the sanitary problems in Tongham on the north side of the Hog's Back. It seems that the authorities still left it to the householder and cottager to dispose of the contents of their buckets and cesspits. The sanitary inspector was concerned, however, that many inhabitants of the village were not doing it properly.

'It is a great mistake to bury sewage deep,' said the good inspector. 'The air cannot get at the sewage, and it will remain undecomposed for months.' He then proceeded to give details of how it should be done: 'A trench not more than 2 inches deep and of sufficient width and about 12 feet in length, will take the contents of an earth pail. This should then be covered with a thin layer of earth. To dispose of the household slops and the contents of the earth pail, not less than 10 rods of ground [one rod equals a length of 16.5 feet] should be available to every six persons.' Unfortunately, out of 129 houses in Tongham only 48 had gardens big enough to enable the occupiers to comply with the sanitary inspector's recommendations.

There were, of course, certain advantages to be gained when the contents of your bucket or cesspit were buried in the garden. 'My grandad just dumped it on the veggy plot and dug it in,' one elderly lady told me. 'He had some prize-winning produce, especially the rhubarb.'

'My uncle at Albury simply tipped the contents of his privy bucket on the manure heap by the pigsties and it eventually ended up on the fields,' recalled Gerald Jarvis.

'The bucket from our privy was emptied into a large covered tank and left to mature,' one Surrey lady told me. 'It was then mixed with water and poured on the garden and fields. Grandfather made his own muck spreader to distribute this concoction. The device needed two people to operate it – one pushing and one pumping. It was a very smelly operation but it did result in some excellent vegetables!'

One version of the bucket privy had a flap in the back wall for removing the bucket, which was emptied either by the owner in the garden or by the night soil men. This method of emptying was not without its problems for privy owners. Mr Cunningham, now living in Grayshott just over the border into Hampshire, wrote to me about a privy of this type at Hindhead: 'About 1948 my friend's mother lived in Beacon Hill and her toilet was several yards up the garden path, next to the shed. Inside was the usual flat board with a hole in the centre of it, and a large bucket underneath. The bucket was emptied and replaced with a clean one through a trap-door at the back of the shed. My friend's mother used to panic in case they took the bucket out when she was sitting there. It did happen to people sometimes!'

Mr Buxton from Merrow spent his childhood at Burnt Common near Send. 'We never had a loo at the bottom of the garden, it was next to the kitchen with a hole in the wall to remove the bucket. It had a door covering the bucket and a small window at the top to let a bit of light and air in, but it was always dark in there. My memories are of summertime in the hot weather when every room in the house had sticky fly papers hanging up. Although most people kept chickens in their gardens, which would attract flies, I realise now where most of the flies came from because our back door was always open.'

Mr Buxton also remembered that the occupiers of houses at Burnt Common had to dispose of their bucket's contents themselves. 'All the dads used to dig a hole in the daytime, but they never emptied the bucket into the hole until night-time. Why the cloak and dagger stuff I don't know because we were all in the same boat!'

Mr Hampshire of Bramley told me about the emptying of his bucket privy at Thorncombe Street, near Hascombe, 60 years ago: 'The men came Sunday night or early Monday morning to empty them. If they were late there was often someone using theirs!'

Brian and Joy Brackley's cesspit privy at Mayford near Woking was emptied via a large flap at the rear. The night soil men came with a large bucket on wheels and the contents of the pit were then ladled into the bucket using a long handled scoop. The brick-built privy still survives, side by side with that belonging to their neighbour, Margaret Smith. At the back of the privy the Brackleys showed me the large arch, now blocked, which gave access to the cesspit.

At Mrs Bache's childhood privy at Worplesdon 'everything went down into a pit. Every now and again the Rural District Council men came to empty it.'

Mrs Grover of Wood Street spent her childhood holidays at her grandparents' in Merrow: 'I remember the newspaper used in the toilet and the candle in the jar to light us on our

Here is the back wall of two 'side by side' brick privies near Woking. The cesspit was emptied via a large single archway, part of which can be seen here at the bottom of the wall. Marks on the wall above the arch show the original position of the hinged flap. (Roy Drysdale)

After the Second World War some privies were converted into chemical loos as I found at Shackleford. (Author)

way – and the draught and smell when the wind cut through the holes in the corrugated cover at the back where the waste was ladled out at night.'

Mr A. J. Cunningham from Canada, but now living in Normandy near Guildford, first came to England during the Second World War but he returned after the end of the war to marry and settle permanently in England. 'Our first home was in Ewhurst,' he wrote. 'At that time there was no main drainage in the village and most cottages had "the little house" at the bottom of the garden. We were quite posh as we had ours in a proper shed. Friends we visited had the usual at the bottom of the garden with a bucket, the contents of which had to be regularly buried in the garden (I couldn't get the hang of that and could never remember where the last one was buried!).'

Anthony Cunningham of Grayshott (no relation to Mr Cunningham of Normandy) warned of the late night dangers for pedestrians in Beacon Hill, Hindhead, even after the Second World War. 'I well remember that if you were about the roads and pavements in the village about 11 o'clock at night, you had to watch out, because some "brave" council man was liable to rush out of a gate carrying a bucket full to the brim. He would be unable to stop it slopping along the pavement before putting it in the back of a special lorry. The smell was incredible! Main drainage came later, much to everyone's relief I think!'

And so say all of us!

[9]

Getting It Down On Paper

I once visited a paper factory and marvelled at the processes that can turn cellulose from wood or even grass into a material so essential to our everyday lives. However, these days most of us only appreciate the luxury of soft toilet tissue when we find, at the moment of our greatest need, that we have run out of it. But what of those times before the shelves of every supermarket had begun to groan under the weight of toilet paper in every imaginable pastel shade?

Ancient man may well have grabbed a handful of grass or leaves to clean himself up. Indeed, dock leaves were still considered a reasonable material for wiping the bottom well into the 20th century. The Romans may indeed have used the ubiquitous sponge on a stick, which was then washed in salt water and left ready for the next user. Such use is said to have given rise to the saying 'getting hold of the wrong end of the stick' but I cannot confirm that. Sticks on their own were used in post-Roman times and this may provide the answer as to the source of the saying. It must have been a mucky and painful experience!

Proper toilet paper arrived in the shops in the middle of the 19th century and in 1880 the British Patent Perforated Paper Company began the manufacture of toilet rolls. Most of us over 40 will remember the slippery and sometimes painfully sharp delights of toilet paper such as Bronco and Izal, which was shiny on one side but less so on the other. It was available in rolls with the paper perforated across every few inches or in interleaved packets of single sheets. The rolls never seemed to tear where you wanted them to! One brand exhorted the user to 'now wash your hands', a message which was repeated at regular intervals throughout the roll.

'Bromo Paper – A Perfectly Pure Article for the Water Closet' was originally imported in packets from the United States but was later manufactured in England by the Diamond Mills Paper Company Ltd.

Bronco toilet paper has, I think, only recently gone out of production. Sad, because I remember as a child the delights of making music with the 'comb and bog paper'. What can we improvising musicians use now?

Bromo, Bronco, or Izal were for those with a little extra cash. The less well off, or those who would rather spend their pennies elsewhere, found a ready made substitute in old newspaper, which left inky marks on thousands of Surrey bottoms. Other sources of paper included magazines, but the glossy paper had obvious disadvantages. Tissue paper was highly prized, especially the wrappings from oranges, whilst some families discovered their own special ways of keeping their bottoms clean.

'*John Bull* and *Pearson's Weekly* were cut into squares and threaded onto a loop of string,' wrote Miss Jordan of Redhill. Perhaps the advantage here was that the ink was less migratory! 'Some time in the late twenties we had the pleasure of using Izal in interleaved sheets in a small packet kept on the side,' she continued. But Miss Jordan's brother seems to have considered that using Izal was not such a pleasure. 'One day my young brother, in a fit of temper, put the whole pack in the bowl. He then had second thoughts, fished it out with a stick and then told Dad that the roof was leaking!'

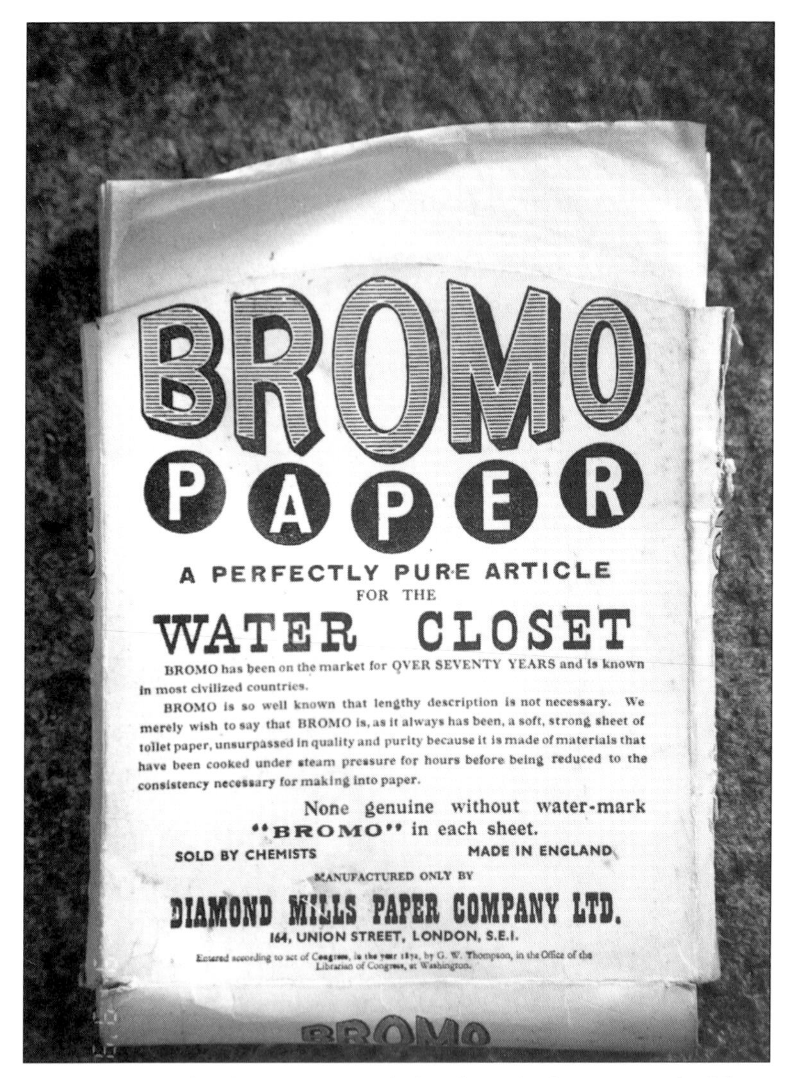

Sheets of 'Bromo' toilet paper came in handy packs. Some examples I have seen boasted the 'highest prize awarded by the Paris Exposition of 1878'. (Len Blackmore)

Mary Gatford's grandfather made a special box decorated with a carving of an owl to house the squares of newspaper. The paper was pulled out through a narrow slot at the bottom of the box but the disadvantage was that each piece of newspaper had to be meticulously cut to the same dimensions in order to fit the box – a very laborious task for a small child. Audrey Creasey also described to me the 'wooden box with neat sizes of newspaper in' at her grandmother's privy near Haslemere. An excellent example of such a box has survived intact in the privy at the National Trust's Oakhurst Cottage at Hambledon.

Many people, like Mary Gatford's grandfather, made their own toilet paper holders but it was not long after the introduction of commercially manufactured paper that holders for rolls and interleaved toilet paper began to appear in local ironmongers. These were originally called toilet fixtures and the British Patent Perforated Paper Company marketed their own toilet roll holder called 'The Cameo'. A connection with royalty seemed important as other examples included the 'Victoria Toilet Fixture' and 'The Crown Toilet Fixture'. There was also 'The Tonbar' manufactured 'in brass with a match holder and tray for spent matches'. At least one company provided 'special rolls of toilet paper which is 500 feet long and is not perforated, as any length from an inch upwards can be instantly detached by means of the patent cutter'. A one inch long piece of toilet paper was surely taking economy too far!

Some families were very resourceful in their search for paper suitable for use in the privy. 'In those days bus and train timetables were big books,' recalled Mary Riddle of Guildford. 'These were cut up and hung on string to use for toilet paper.

The British Patent Perforated Paper Company (BPPP Co) also supplied toilet roll holders or 'toilet fixtures' as they were called. (Len Blackmore)

Many of the people who wrote to me or telephoned remembered as children being given the task of cutting or tearing up old newspapers into squares for the privy. During the Second World War the pages featuring Hitler or Mussolini were particularly popular! For Mr Trower of Farley Green this was a task for the winter evenings.

Mr S. Jones from Shere wrote a prize-winning poem about his early days in Peaslake, which appeared in a little book entitled *I Remember When*, which I helped to publish in 1995. Two verses are particularly appropriate here:

I did some jobs for my old mum
Round about the house,
From chopping up the fire wood,
To maybe, catch a mouse.

But there was one job I didn't like
And wasn't it a caper,
Sitting there with scissors
Making toilet paper.

An 'old soldier' told me that, during his years in the forces, when a requisition was put in for toilet paper it was always known as 'Army Form Blank', as opposed to the myriad of numbered forms produced by the Army, which might just as well have been used in the loo. He also told me about a Company Sergeant Major at Pirbright, who was most concerned about the huge volume of toilet paper being used by the soldiers in his 'care'.

'You only need three pieces at a time!' he bawled out to the troops. 'One up! One down! And one to polish!'

An interesting early outside flush loo at Whyteleafe with a plain stoneware bowl with lid and a local cistern. (Mary Pritchard)

[10]

The Best Years Of Your Life

Most of us have not particularly pleasant memories of school loos. Even when they flushed I can remember that they were always in a separate building behind the school. They were draughty, very smelly and freezing cold, literally, in winter. Unfriendly places where you ventured as little as possible and in class waited, sometimes in desperation, for the bell that told you school was over for the day. But worst of all was that the authorities seemed too mean to put any locks on the doors! This left the desperate pupil very vulnerable to the school prankster or the bullies.

Most of Surrey's rural schools had loos with buckets or cesspits until well after the Second World War. These were regularly emptied by the night soil men from the local council, usually via trap doors on the outside of the back wall of the privy block. I visited Ewhurst School with local historian Janet Balchin, where the original toilet block is still in use, though now with flush facilities. However, the blocked arches, once covered by hinged trap doors, through which the men extracted the buckets could still be clearly seen.

Hascombe School closed in 1964 and has been converted into five dwellings, but the boys' toilet block still stands. Tile hung, with gables and mainly built of local Bargate stone, it is now used for storage by Mrs Reed, who lives in the adjacent part of the old school. It is a wonderful looking little building, far superior to any of the utilitarian constructions I had to use as a child, but none of the original internal features survive. I doubt if any of the boys who used it gave

The loos at Ewhurst School are still used but fortunately they have been fully converted to flush. However, the four arched orifices through which the privy buckets were removed for emptying, although now blocked, can clearly be seen at the bottom of the back wall. (Roy Drysdale)

any thought to the architectural merits of their loos.

In her book *Memories of Hambledon*, Mary Parker described the privies at her village school: 'There was no indoor sanitation – just six wooden sentry boxes in the playground, with buckets in them, three for the boys and three for the girls, and these were looked after by Mr Dedman who, with his wife, was caretaker of the school for 15 years.'

Chiddingfold School had bucket privies – two for the boys and two for the girls – and these were emptied via the usual outside trap doors. Unfortunately, the girls had to be very careful when they settled down upon the seat. According to Joan Hardy, it was not unusual for some of the boys to hide at

The quaintly designed boys' loo block at the now closed Hascombe School has survived as a storage shed. (Roy Drysdale)

the back of the loos armed with a bunch of stinging nettles. They waited until one of the girls was in situ and then lifted the trap door and poked the nettles through the hole to brush against the defenceless bottom.

Edward Lucas heard a similar story from his father: 'I remember my father telling me the toilets at his school had several seats back to back over the stream. One side was for the girls, the other for the boys. When a new pupil came to use a seat, some rascal was delegated to enter the other side with a leafy stick, make it wet and dust the newcomer's bottom. Those outside watched, hoping the victim would dash out with clothes down, which some newcomers did sometimes!'

Wood Street: the Growth of a Village, published by Wood Street

The staff toilet block at the Wrecclesham Pottery near Farnham is roofed with green-glazed tiles manufactured on site. Apparently, the tiles were the leftovers from an order which went to roof a bank in Rangoon in Burma! (Chris Shepheard/Farnham Buildings Preservation Trust)

Village History Society, described the state of the village school in 1904: '72 children were housed in the extension and 23 infants in the original classroom. The toilets were of the hopper type with no water available for flushing (they were flushed and cleaned once a week with water carried from the house well). The cesspools were emptied twice a year, usually at night, by men with buckets.'

Mr Buxton of Merrow remembered his school privies and how he found out who emptied them: 'The school my twin brother and I went to in Send was a normal C of E village school. We had, I think, ten privies, six for the girls and four for the boys, divided by a wall. They were situated about 150 feet from the school at the end of the playground, which was alright in the summertime but a bit grim in the winter. The buckets were emptied every day and they were scrubbed and cleaned and I never ever remember them smelling. I suppose we just took it for granted.

'One day the headmaster wanted to know if any of us older boys had air rifles. We didn't know why so we all kept quiet until he explained that he wanted some of us to go early in the morning to shoot pigeons, which were raiding the gardens. My brother and I had air guns and a couple of other lads had them as well. We got there about half six in the morning and solved the mystery of who emptied the buckets. It was the school cleaner – a lady who looked old to us lads but I suppose she was about 50. We knew who she was from the village but never knew that it was her job. I must admit that we took the mick out of her two younger children, who went to the school. Kids can be very cruel!'

[11]

Other Uses

For many people the privy was not a place where you tarried for long, especially after sunset. 'When I spent my holidays at Pirbright the one thing that terrified me was having to use the loo at night when it was dark,' said Marie Kite.

'If you had to go up the garden in the evening, it was a bit eerie, walking along with a torch, all quiet, suddenly an owl or fox would screech out and nearly frighten the life out of you!' said Mr Cunningham.

'There was a rough ceiling where many spiders seemed to dwell – a frightening experience to me, wondering if I would have one drop on my head!' recalled Miss Jordan.

'I was sometimes frightened by strange rustling noises but usually it turned out only to be birds in the ivy on the roof,' said Doris Vincent. But wildlife in the privy could sometimes be very real!

'If you went to the loo after dark with a lantern,' recalled my neighbour, 'it was always advisable to kick the door before going in to get rid of any rats.'

'For the first 17 years of my life I lived in a farm cottage with no modern sanitation,' wrote June Spong of Dorking. 'We washed at the kitchen sink, bathed in front of the fire and had a gazunder under the bed. The earth closet was at the back of the wood shed and if you looked up at the ceiling, you could see the rats peeping over the edge and looking at you!'

I found this privy in a dark corner of a derelict stable block near Ewhurst. No privacy here for the stable lads! (Roy Drysdale)

However, a properly cared for privy need not be a smelly hole filled with unspeakable horrors, real or imaginary. 'My mother kept our privy beautifully clean and scrubbed. I never remember it being smelly,' wrote one correspondent. In these circumstances a privy could become a place of quiet contemplation. 'Dad used to spend hours in there, humming to himself and reading the squares of newspaper – not always very nice when you were getting a bit desperate yourself!'

Mary Gatford remembers that her father and grandfather often used to sit together in their three-holer for 'important discussions'. She also recalled that the privy was a useful place in which to hide if you were in trouble!

The privy was also a quiet place for a smoke. This was proved to me a few years ago when I helped on a small archaeological 'dig' in Godalming. The main 'feature' we discovered turned out to be the pit for a privy. It was full of crumbly lumps of what appeared to be lime, which had obviously been thrown into the pit to treat the contents. The passage of many years meant that digging it out was not a smelly occupation at all! We found that 'fossilized' into the lumps of lime there were a large number of clay tobacco pipes which had, no doubt, been dropped down the hole following a contemplative smoke. Incidentally, there were also pieces of newspaper in the lumps dating from the late 1870s!

Privy owners often hung pictures in their 'dunnys' to make them more homely and it was not unknown for a small library to be housed in there! Lighting and heating could be a problem but some people managed to overcome this. Joy

Brackley bought a little oil lamp for 6d from Woolworths and at night this was kept lit in their privy at Woking. 'It not only meant that you could see what you were doing but it also kept the little room surprisingly warm. It didn't cost much in oil to keep it burning all night.'

Mrs Bache remembers using candles and 'an Aladdin lamp, which was an oil lamp with a mantle, which gave quite a good light really'. Many people I spoke to had memories of the candle in a jar which could produce ghostly flickering shadows on the walls and ceiling of the privy.

As a child Evelyn Browne lived in Farncombe. 'We had a little toilet at the bottom of our garden but I used to love to get down there, no matter what the weather. I used to sit on that little wooden seat with the door open for ages. The simple reason for this was that there was a pigeon loft in front of me, and I used to sit mesmerised by the pigeons. They would nest, lay their eggs which would eventually hatch, and I just loved to watch them hatch into little babies and then until they grew up. And so it went on.

'The privy was horrid in winter time but in the summer it was a good place to hide while we ate the plums we stole from the orchard,' wrote Audrey Creasey.

Some privies I discovered had wonderful views across fields and hills. The owner of a privy built on the top of a hill at Shackleford must surely have sat there with the door open and admired the miles of beautiful green rolling Surrey countryside visible from the seat!

The privy could also be a secret place for romance as June Spong remembers. June sometimes stayed at her future husband's farmhouse home and when, in the night, the call of nature became too strong she 'would have to wake George, who was sleeping in the next bedroom. We would don overcoats, walk along a long corridor, down a wide flight of polished stairs, out of the back door, around the house, through the gardens and over the stream via the rickety bridge to the privy, where George stood guard outside. Then there was the thought of the journey back again, only to find that sleep was not on our minds as we were now wide awake!' They soon discovered that the remote privy was a quiet place for a 'kiss and cuddle' during the day. Marie Kite of Pirbright also found the privy a good place for 'hugs and kisses', when she visited her fiancé's bungalow at Pirbright.

A block of four privies at Farncombe – very sociable! (Roy Drysdale)

Many privies were grouped in blocks to serve, for example, a row of cottages and here there was the unavoidable opportunity to meet your neighbours as Mr Hampshire of Bramley recalled. 'I went to live at Cheyne Row, Thorncombe Street, 60 years ago. Newly married, I had been used to flush toilets and now there were five bucket toilets facing the back doors. It took me weeks to get used to them, not too bad when I got to know my neighbours. It was hard to pretend that you were not in there and easier to have a conversation with the person next door as to what you had eaten the day before, or whether you had taken your Beecham Powder!'

Unfortunately, the privy could also be a dangerous place as a result of other people's mischief. Mary Gatford's grandfather found this out the hard way. 'One dark night my brother, seeing grandfather going down to the privy, decided to play a trick. He waited until grandfather was well ensconced. He then went to the back of the privy, lit some newspaper, lifted the flap and tossed the flaming paper in. Suddenly there was what seemed like a huge explosion and in a flash grandfather was out the door with his trousers round his ankles, yelling pure murder!'

'Using the toilet at the garage near Haslemere where I worked during the 1950s could be dangerous sometimes as someone from the garage was very likely to whip open the trap door and "lob" a brick into the bucket when you were sitting there! But I got round the problem by always parking a car in front of the trap door, locking the car and keeping the keys with me in the privy!' wrote Anthony Cunningham.

Some Surrey privies are now on their last legs! (Roy Drysdale)

But others lovingly cared for. Note that this is another Surrey privy supporting a nest box. (Roy Drysdale)

In wartime there were other dangers that threatened those in the process of seeking relief in the privy, as Miss Jordan related: 'In 1940 a German plane dropped a delayed action bomb in our garden at Redhill. It exploded after the "all clear" had been sounded, along with another one dropped in an adjoining road. Seven houses were destroyed. My mother, having just used the loo, had hold of the door to close it at the exact moment when the bomb exploded. The sizeable yew hedge surrounding the privy saved her from being buried, but she was blown across the yard. All this happened at 11.20 at night.'

D. J. Buxton's privy near Send was replaced by a flush loo in 1939 but this strategic improvement soon became a target for the enemy. It was eventually flattened by a flying bomb in 1944.

However, another of Mary Gatford's experiences might be described as 'the enemy within'. When her father built a new bungalow for the family he also had to build the privy. Having a little gunpowder in his possession he decided to take a short cut and he blew a hole in the ground! 'What a huge hole it was! He shored it up with timbers and put further timbers across the top and built a little brick house above it. The hole was so big it didn't need cleaning out very often! For the inside facilities father used an oblong porcelain toilet decorated with roses. We called the privy the "bottoms house", but I didn't like it. I had a terrible vision of the floor boards giving way and me falling into the huge hole! For that reason I never stayed long in the "bottoms house"!'

Two sets of back-to-back privies down the garden path at Ewhurst. (Roy Drysdale)

I suppose I could say that we have just about run out of paper so, to avoid any embarrassment, I will end my journey down the garden path here. I hope that you have enjoyed my book wherever you may have read it. Perhaps, if you're in the little room at this moment, this book may save your blushes, but do keep the pages with the pictures!

A Privy By Any Other Name

The name 'privy' comes from the Old French word *privé*, which in turn was derived from the Latin *privatus* meaning private. The privy and the act of visiting it have been given a variety of names over the years. Here are a few that I have come across during my 'privy hunts' in Surrey.

Bog
Boghouse
Bottoms House
Closet
Comfort station
Crapphouse
Dunnikin
Dunny
Dyke
Funny Place
Gang
Garderobe
Go and see a man about a dog
Going to drop a packet
Going to powder my nose
Going to spend a penny
Going to the how's your father
Gong
Have a Jimmy Riddle
Have a Tom Tit
Holy of holies
Jakes
Jericho
Karzi
Latrine
Lav
Lavatory
Little House
Little room
Loo
Place of easement
Plumbing
Reading room
Shit Hole
Shithouse
Stoolroom
The George
The John
The throne room
Wotyermacallit
Yer Tiz
Yer Twas but t'ain't no more (after they moved the outside 'gents' inside at my local pub!)